CRIME AND PUNISHMENT

Changing Attitudes 1900–2000

Alison Brownlie

RAINTREE
STECK-VAUGHN
PUBLISHERS
A Steck-Vaughn Company

Austin, Texas
www.steck-vaughn.com

TWENTIETH CENTURY ISSUES SERIES

Published by Raintree Steck-Vaughn Publishers, an imprint of Steck-Vaughn Company

Library of Congress Cataloging-in-Publication Data
Brownlie, Alison.
Crime and punishment / Alison Brownlie.
     p.   cm.—(20th Century Issues)
     Includes bibliographical references and index.
     Summary: Explains how attitudes toward both crime and punishment have changed throughout the twentieth century, discussing organized crime, political crimes, policing, the judicial system, punishment and prison, and the internationalization of crime.
     ISBN 0-8172-5573-7
     1. Criminal investigation—History—
Juvenile literature.
     [1. Crime—History. 2. Criminal investigation—
History.]
     I. Title.
     HV8073.8.B76   1999
     364—dc21   99-26777

Printed in Italy. Bound in the United States.
1 2 3 4 5 6 7 8 9 0 04 03 02 01 00

Picture acknowledgments
Corbis-Bettmann: 5 (Everett/Corbis), 8, 10, 15 (Reuters), 19 (UPI), 23 (UPI), 24, 35, 43 (Reuters), 44, 47 (UPI), 52 (UPI), 53 (UPI), 54; Mary Evans Picture Library: 6, 26, 28, 30, 32, 48, 49; Hulton Getty Picture Collection: 58; Impact: 9 (Rhonda Klevansky), 11 (Marco Siqueira), 25 (Christopher Pillitz), 55 (Oleg Lastochkin/Vika); Panos Pictures: 40 (Sean Sprague), 57 (Betty Press), 59 (Chris Stowers); Popperfoto: 7, 21 (Reuters), 29 (Reuters), 38 (Reuters), 39 (Reuters), 42 (Reuters), 45 (Reuters), 46 (Reuters), 50; Topham Picturepoint: 4, 13, 16, 20 (Associated Press), 27, 31, 34, 51, 56; Wayland Picture Library: 9, 11, 22, 33, 36, 37, 41;

Cover: main picture shows a boot camp in the United States (Corbis-Bettmann/UPI); black-and-white pictures show, top to bottom, Louise Masset being hanged, Newgate, London, 1900 (Mary Evans Picture Library); Al Capone (Wayland Picture Library); Arrest of Mafia boss Pietro Aglieri, June 1997 (Popperfoto).

CRIME AND PUNISHMENT IN THE TWENTIETH CENTURY

In the broadest legal sense, a crime in most countries is an act committed that breaks the law of that country. Courts may impose a variety of punishments against those who commit crimes, including a fine, imprisonment, or death. For as long as there have been rules about how society should be run, people have committed crimes. Notings of crimes, such as murder and theft, date back to when records began.

Elderly people are particularly fearful of becoming the victims of street crime. This eighty-one-year-old woman was knocked to the ground when she refused to hand over her bag to a teenage mugger.

Many types of crimes that were committed long ago are still committed today. But with changes in technology and in society as a whole, criminals have developed new ways of committing crimes. And society has devised new methods and techniques with which to catch them.

When a criminal is found guilty of a crime, that criminal is punished. Until relatively recently, it was felt that the punishment meted out to the criminal should atone for the crime. It was not generally believed that punishment should also improve the chances of the criminal's eventually fitting back into society. During the past hundred years, debates have raged about the role and nature of punishment for convicted criminals.

CRIME AS ENTERTAINMENT

For many years, crime has been the major focus of much of our leisure and entertainment industry—it is the subject of many popular movies, television dramas, and books. In the United States, crime and law enforcement programs account for about a third of total television output. But crime is also a source of great anxiety. People worry about being victims of crime, and much publicity is devoted to whether criminals receive appropriate or adequate punishment.

Crime fascinates us, but it is also a source of fear. The elderly are particularly fearful of some kinds of crime and feel that they are vulnerable targets for criminals when out on the streets. People spend huge amounts of money on house alarms and sophisticated security systems. Crime statistics, however, do not bear out certain commonly accepted fears. For example, it is not women, children, or the elderly who are most at risk: young men are far more likely to be victims, particularly of violent crimes.

OPINION

"We're barking mad about crime in this country. We have an obsession with believing the worst, conning ourselves that there was a golden age—typically forty years before the one we're living in."
Nick Ross, broadcaster and host of BBC TV's *Crime Watch* program.

A scene from the film Reservoir Dogs. *Some critics have accused such movies of glamorizing violence and crime.*

A pickpocket at a racetrack in Paris around 1890. If no resistance is offered, pickpocketing is treated as theft or larceny; but it is treated as robbery if the victim puts up a fight.

How well-founded are our concerns about crime today? Many people would argue that crime has increased dramatically during the century and that the situation is almost out of control. They hark back to a "safer" era in history, when there was greater respect for people and property. But at the beginning of the twentieth century, there were huge concerns about crime. Victorian London was infamous for its fantastically high levels of prostitution, petty thieving, street crime, and child crime.

The fact that crime is more widely reported probably contributes to the public perception that there is currently a worldwide epidemic of lawlessness. Before 1950, most people in the Western world depended on the limited news coverage provided by radio, newspapers, and movie newsreels. During the 1950s and 1960s, nearly every home in the Western world suddenly had access to a television set. And, as a result of the technological revolution of the past twenty years, people now have virtually unlimited access to information about crime through the press, television, and even the Internet. Newspaper coverage of crimes has become so extensive that there have been occasions when it has jeopardized a person's right to a fair trial (for example, in cases when pretrial information is released that might prejudice the members of a jury).

Meanwhile, in many parts of the world, crime is virtually unknown or negligible. In Samoa, an island state in the Pacific, there is a little weekend alcohol-related crime, and in Brunei in Southeast Asia, a stolen car often makes television news headlines. In some other countries, the crime rate is falling. In Argentina, crime fell by one-fourth in 1992: this was possibly a reflection of the country's increasing political and economic stability (although crime is still rife in the poorer shantytown areas). Even in Japan, a modern industrialized country, crime rates are lower than in Great Britain or the United States.

A police escort outside a bank in Brunei. Brunei's low crime rate is largely attributable to the state of emergency that has been in force since 1962, giving the government the power to detain without charge or trial for indefinite renewable two-year periods.

ATTITUDES TOWARD PUNISHMENT

There is a range of ideas about the different types of punishment meted out to criminals. Many people hold strong views about crime and punishment, views that reflect their basic attitudes toward other humans and how much they believe that criminals are responsible for their actions. Some people believe that crime is an illness, so punishment should take the form of a cure. This belief assumes that people are not able to take responsibility for their actions. Others feel that we must all be accountable for what we do and that punishment exists to remind us of our social responsibilities.

For much of history, people believed that punishment should be harsh and brutal, and there was little sympathy for the criminal. However, in the nineteenth century a movement dedicated to improving and reforming conditions in prisons gained momentum and some popularity. Liberal ideas about crime and punishment were aired in a number of popular novels, such as *Les Miserables* by Victor Hugo and *Crime and Punishment* by Fyodor Mikhailovich Dostoevsky. These books encouraged people to think more deeply about why society punishes criminals. In the second half of the nineteenth century, the idea that a jail sentence should reform prisoners as well as punish them began to gain support.

Public floggings in Iran, such as this one, probably in the 1930s, still take place for more than a hundred offenses. Executions are common for political "crimes."

During the twentieth century, attitudes toward punishment have fluctuated. Sometimes the view that punishment should be harsh and tough prevails; at other times there is greater emphasis on the reform of criminals for the greater good of society as a whole. These fluctuations from one extreme to another are often a reaction to what has gone before. It is possible to judge whether a certain policy has succeeded or not only when it has been applied over a number of years. So the successes and failures of policies on punishment can be assessed only with the benefit of hindsight.

CRIME AND INSTABILITY

Do any particular events and circumstances result in an increase in crime? It is difficult to draw conclusions because even criminologists do not always agree about the factors that affect the crime rate. However, during wars and the aftereffects of war, and in periods of political and economic instability, crime does seem to flourish. During World War II, crime levels among young people in Great Britain increased dramatically. In 1991, after the Gulf War, sanctions were imposed by the Western allies on Iraq. This led to the collapse of the Iraqi economy and a soaring crime rate in what had previously been a law-abiding society. For most of the twentieth century, South Africa was controlled by a white minority government that, under a system called apartheid, treated the black majority population as second-class citizens. There was violence and high criminality. However, since the ending of apartheid in the early 1990s, South Africa has seen its crime rate soar.

Totalitarianism is a form of government particular to the twentieth century. Totalitarian states, such as that of Germany under Adolf Hitler, the USSR under Josef Stalin, and China under Mao Zedong, kept crime rates low through what may be described as "policing by terror." The use of secret

> ### OPINION
>
> In Great Britain, in 1966, Myra Hindley was sentenced to life imprisonment for a series of child murders. Under British law, "life imprisonment" usually means release after eight to ten years, but successive officials have decided that Hindley should remain behind bars indefinitely. One official, Michael Howard, suggested that, in her case, "life" should mean life. Hindley's case draws attention to the question about whether a life sentence should literally mean life or should mean the length of time it takes for a criminal to be "reformed" in prison.

The massive increase in crime in South Africa since the end of apartheid has led people to take stringent measures to protect themselves and their homes from break-ins.

OPINION

The Greek philosopher Aristotle (384–322 B.C.) said "Poverty is the parent of revolution and crime."

KEY MOMENT

In December 1991, Mikhail Gorbachev resigned as president of the USSR. His resignation led to the end of Communist rule in the Soviet Union. The introduction of greater democracy, along with free market capitalism, is thought by some to have created instability and chaos in this once authoritarian society. Throughout the former Soviet Union, Mafia-style gangs have exploited the situation and are engaging in widespread drug-dealing and extortion. To date, a number of politicians, police officers, and Mafia opponents have been murdered.

police, high levels of surveillance, and harsh punishment were effective in deterring crime, but at the price of personal freedom and freedom of speech. In particular, it was a crime to speak out against the government or its policies. The notion of what constitutes a crime in a totalitarian regime is different from the idea of what constitutes a crime in a democratic society. In totalitarian states most people live in fear of harsh punishment by government agents and by the secret police.

THE NEW UNDERCLASS

Throughout the nineteenth and twentieth centuries, huge numbers of people have left the countryside to seek work and a better life in towns and cities. Today, this trend is particularly acute in developing countries. It has resulted in a rapid growth of cities and the percentage of the world's population who live in them. However, only a few people manage to find the riches they seek. Many struggle to make ends meet and are forced into a lifestyle based on

Early in the twentieth century, New York City crime rates were fantastically high. In some slum districts, murder was an everyday occurrence.

something called the "informal economy." This means running businesses outside the normal framework of laws and regulations and not paying taxes. This is often regarded as a criminal offense. In countries like Brazil, an increasing number of abandoned children live out their lives on the streets and resort to crime in order to survive.

The exodus from country to city is a significant factor in the growing divide between the rich and the poor. People have long believed that poverty and inequality are the fundamental causes of crime. Statistics seem to show that in economically prosperous countries, with a relatively small disparity between rich and poor and where the government has the support of its people, there is relatively less crime.

OPINION

Burma is currently ruled by a totalitarian military government. In 1990, Aung San Suu Kyi was elected as the country's leader in a democratic election that the military regime immediately declared void. She was placed under house detention for six years. The military regime regards her as a criminal, although she is regarded as a heroine by many in the West. She believes strongly in human rights: "... even those who do not believe in human rights," she says, "must certainly agree that the rule of law is most important; without the rule of law there can be no peace.... In Burma, at the moment, there is no rule of law."

Street children arrested for robbery in the Brazilian city of Rio de Janeiro. They can expect no special treatment because they are children, however. Many children come to Rio from the impoverished northeast of the country.

Throughout the century, the world has changed rapidly and in many ways. These changes are reflected in the different crimes that are committed and in how those who offend are punished. This book will look at the history of crime over the past hundred years and will examine the range of punishments meted out in response.

THE CHANGING FACE OF CRIME

The list of deeds considered to be crimes is constantly changing. For example, in Christian countries heresy, or the holding of beliefs that oppose the teachings of a particular religion, used to be a crime punishable by death. This no longer applies, although in countries such as Iran and Sudan, Kharjite heresy (opposition to the teachings of orthodox Islam) has recently become a punishable offense.

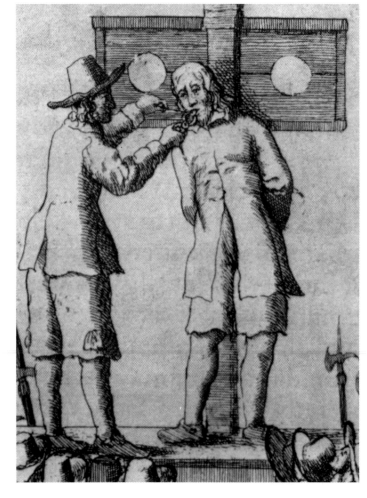

In seventeenth-century Great Britain, physical punishment was the norm. A religious fanatic, James Naylor, had his tongue cut out as part of his punishment.

12

As attitudes toward crime change, so do the crimes themselves. In New York City at the beginning of the twentieth century, it was illegal to spit in public or for women to smoke tobacco. These activities are no longer illegal in New York, but in Singapore today heavy fines are imposed on people caught chewing gum or dropping litter in public. And crimes exist today that were unheard of at the start of the twentieth century. In many countries, the pollution of air and water is now a punishable offense, and new laws have been proposed to deal with the massive increase in the use, and abuse, of computers.

CRIME RATES

Crime statistics are notoriously difficult to gather and are open to different interpretations. Crime rates can rise and fall inexplicably, making it hard to see what the overall trend is. Over the century as a whole, the rate appears to have risen, but this does not necessarily mean an increase in crime; it may simply be that more crimes are being reported to the police or that there are more laws to be broken. If the rates are indeed increasing, it is probably a reflection of the weakening of informal controls in society—parents, school, church, and neighbors. We would expect things to go on getting worse as the development of more technologically sophisticated economies increases the pool of poor, socially excluded young men. However, most recently, crime appears to be falling in many developed countries. Some argue that the increasing use of technology in crime detection and control is enabling enforcement agencies to stay just one step ahead of the criminal.

Often the trends are different for different crimes. In most Western countries, theft and robbery have apparently increased

New technology adds to the range of ways in which crimes can be committed. Here computer equipment used to create false bank cards and credit cards is being checked out by a detective.

dramatically over the century, although the general rate of increase for all crime is only around five percent per year, and the murder rate has decreased. The increase in property crime may be partially attributable to the fact that, as people have become more affluent during the century, they own more that is worth stealing. Computer theft currently accounts for over a fifth of all burglaries in the United States.

CAR CRIMES

The invention of the autombile and its increasingly widespread use throughout the century has spawned offenses that range from speeding to car theft, joy-riding, drunken driving, and road rage. By 1925, there were 20 million cars registered in the United States. In that year, the traffic director of Washington, D.C., threatened to reduce the speed limit to 22 mph, following the death in a traffic accident of a four-year-old boy. In 1932, the British Parliament approved a bill that made motorists who killed people in road accidents guilty of manslaughter. Toward the end of the century, the phenomenon of "road rage"—aggressive behavior by motorists in response to the actions of other road users—has in some cases led to serious assaults and even murder. And incidences of car theft are phenomenally high in all Western countries.

A young man being breathalyzed after a serious traffic accident. Most countries now consider drunken driving a serious crime.

DRUGS AND CRIME

It is true that drugs have had an enormous impact on the world of crime in the twentieth century. Many of the drugs in circulation today have been known for thousands of years. Some now illegal drugs were once freely available. For example, during the nineteenth century parents would often give their children a mixture of alcohol and opium (known as laudanum) to help them sleep. Laudanum was available from pharmacists on demand in most of Europe and North America.

KEY MOMENT

Synthesizing drugs

In 1943, a Swiss chemist named Albert Hofmann created a substance he called lysergic acid diethylamide, or LSD. The invention of LSD heralded a new era of synthetically produced drugs. In the 1960s young people discovered how to make it themselves, and the widespread use of LSD became a key feature of the hippie culture.

Dutch youths selling marijuana cigarettes with a multilanguage sign on a street in Amsterdam. Sales of soft drugs in cafes are tolerated by the authorities in the Netherlands.

However, during the twentieth century, greater awareness of the harmful effects of drugs meant that in most countries drugs used for recreational purposes were made illegal. Today, although many drugs are illegal in their own right, they are linked to crimes in other ways. People commit crimes under the influence of drugs because they feel less inhibited. Some people are often driven to commit crimes such as theft and burglary to get the money they need to buy drugs to feed their habit. Others become involved in the illegal smuggling of, and dealing in, drugs. A large minority of property crime, perhaps up to one-third in Great Britain, is believed to be drug-related.

Mick Jagger and Keith Richards leaving the Chichester law court in May 1967, after being accused of offenses under England's Dangerous Drugs Act.

Drug trafficking, or the illegal manufacture and sale of controlled substances, has become a highly profitable activity. Smuggling is carried out by "couriers" working for a variety of international organized crime groups— the Italian Mafia and Camorra groups, the Chinese triads, and the Medellin cartel, among others (see Chapter 3). Efforts to limit drug trafficking have been ineffective, thwarted by corruption (often at very high levels) and by the law of supply and demand.

As early as 1914, the Harrison Act was passed in the United States. This was the first legislation against the illegal flow of narcotics into the country. But soon organized gangs such as the Mafia began dealing in drug and did much to spread their use and subsequent addictions. By the 1960s, the use of drugs was endemic. In 1967, members of the rock group the Rolling Stones were in court on drugs charges, and in 1970 the cult figure and former Harvard psychology professor Dr. Timothy Leary was sentenced to ten years' imprisonment for smuggling marijuana.

In the Netherlands, possession of small amounts of so-called soft drugs (such as marijuana) has the legal status of a petty offense, and it is usually disregarded by the police. Some feel that this approach breaks the link between relatively safe and relatively dangerous drugs and means that fewer people acquire criminal convictions for minor offenses. Many would argue that severe antidrug laws perpetuate organized crime. Certainly, when drug consignments are successfully intercepted by the authorities, it drives up the street value of the drugs and creates a vacuum, which traffickers rush to fill.

MURDER

Universally, murder is the most serious of crimes. Whereas some crimes, such as drug use or gambling, are considered criminal because society seeks to regulate these particular types of behavior, murder is considered as wrong in itself and inherently evil. But despite the very high profile given to murder cases on the news and in movies, the rate of murder has declined in the long run and is currently stable. There is evidence to suggest that the risk of being murdered in Great Britain has halved every hundred years since the thirteenth century.

Some criminologists believe that the motives for committing murders have altered during the last hundred years. Most of the infamous Victorian murders were for gain and associated with robbery. In 1888 the apparently motiveless murder by "Jack the Ripper" of five London prostitutes signified the beginning of a new age of attacks on women accompanied by rape and murder. By the 1940s murders such as these had become more commonplace. However, many murders take place in the home, and in the United States it is estimated that at least 30 percent of women who are murdered are killed by someone they know, most often a husband or boyfriend.

A CRIMINAL TYPE?

Criminology is the scientific study of crime and criminal behavior. Criminologists search for the causes of criminal behavior in the hope that the information they uncover will be used to limit crime. In the late nineteenth century, the Italian psychiatrist and anthropologist Cesare Lombroso embarked on a detailed study of convicts. He wanted to discover whether criminal behavior was biologically determined—in other words, whether there was a criminal gene that could be inherited.

KEY MOMENT

Dunblane
The horrific killing of sixteen young children by a lone gunman at a primary school in Dunblane, Scotland, on March 13, 1996, led the British government to introduce restrictive gun legislation. Similar acts of violence in Tasmania, Australia, and the United States have renewed calls in those countries for tougher gun control.

Lombroso's findings were highly influential, so much so that at the beginning of the twentieth century the common view was that some people were just born criminals. Some believed that you could identify criminals by their physical appearance and that people who committed different crimes each had their own "look." Swindlers, for example, were overweight with large jaws, prominent cheekbones, and pale faces; pickpockets were tall with long hands, black hair, and scanty beards. During the twentieth century, as people became aware of the role played by social factors such as poverty, upbringing, and opportunity in creating a criminal, Lombroso's view of the criminal type was refuted. However, scientists are now investigating whether one's DNA may include a predilection for some sorts of crime, an echo of the idea around at the beginning of the century that a tendency toward crime is possibly congenital.

JUVENILE CRIME

As the century has advanced, more and more crimes have been committed by young people. Juvenile delinquency is now a major social problem. In the aftermath of World War II, many thought that juvenile delinquency was a result of a worldwide change in social order. However, youth crime had clearly existed earlier in the century, too. Some argue that, with the advent of the welfare state in Great Britain, better records were kept of youth crime, so there appeared to be more of it. However, the statistics are alarming. In New York City, by 1957, youths under the age of eighteen comprised 50 percent of those arrested for robbery and 60 percent of those arrested for burglary. In the same year in Los Angeles, a fifth of all crimes were committed by people under eighteen. Between 1960 and 1978, the number of juvenile court cases rose 166 percent in the United States, and the rate continues to rise. This trend is reflected in all countries and is universally attributed to the fundamental change in traditional patterns of family life and community.

Persistent juvenile offenders are likely to come from a background of poverty and tend to live in an urban area. Racial or ethnic groups that experience discrimination may also produce young people who express delinquent behavior. Criminologists who study juvenile delinquency attempt to explain it in various ways. One theory is that children from the poorest part of society lack opportunities to develop in socially acceptable ways and turn to delinquency as a substitute. Another theory is that delinquency is learned by associating with people who have little respect for the law. A third explanation points to biological causes or emotional and psychological distress. All these theories are, to some extent, valid.

The twentieth century has seen a heightened awareness of certain acts that previously received little attention and were often not reported, especially crimes such as rape and domestic violence against women. In the second half of the century, support groups have encouraged women to report these crimes and have put pressure on the police to take them more seriously. Society as a whole has become more aware of child abuse and pedophilia, and people are more prepared now to report their suspicions to the police. Some crimes—"date rape" and "stalking" for example— have been more clearly defined and publicized. This greater emphasis on crimes against the person (as opposed to crimes against property) has been a persistent feature of late twentieth-century life.

In the latter part of the century, more prominence has been given to violent crimes against women. Here, at a press conference in 1978, Mary Vincent, age 15, warns young people not to hitchhike. She describes how she was picked up by a motorist who raped her and cut off her arms with an ax.

ORGANIZED CRIME

Organized crime is an enterprise, involving a number of people working closely together, whose purpose is to gain profit and power by engaging in primarily illegal activities. Members of organized criminal gangs operate within a hierarchical structure and are willing to use violence or bribery (often both) to achieve their ends. Violence and threats of violence are also used to maintain the discipline and secrecy of organized criminal activities. Organized crime has grown throughout the twentieth century, and today it is sophisticated, technologically advanced, and international: it is big business. As such, it presents one of the greatest challenges for the maintenance of law and order in the next century.

In times of economic and political instability, when people are often forced to adopt any means of providing for themselves and their families and the resources to tackle crime are lacking, gangs of criminals move in rapidly to exploit the situation. Examples of this can be seen today all over the world, particularly in South Africa and the former Soviet Union.

A hallmark of the Mafia is its readiness to resort to extremes of violence and intimidation. In May 1992 the Italian judge Giovanni Falcone, who was investigating Mafia crimes, was murdered in a huge car bomb attack. His wife, Francesca, and three police officers were killed along with him.

A WORLDWIDE PHENOMENON

However, nearly every country has, or has had, some element of organized crime. Japan, a country with one of the lowest crime rates in the world, nevertheless has organized gangs of criminals known as the kumi, whose members are called yakuza. There are also the Chinese triads, the Neapolitan Camorra, Sicilian Mafia, and Colombian and Mexican crime "families." Increasingly, young people are becoming involved in group or gang criminal activity. In Los Angeles, Manila, Tokyo, and New York, small groups roam the streets carrying out petty thievery and muggings for money to buy drugs.

This chapter focuses on the way in which organized crime has burgeoned into a multimillion dollar international business and how criminals have adapted their activities to suit the political and economic circumstances.

Two police officers inspect part of a load of marijuana confiscated in the Colombian port of Cartagena in May 1998. The total haul, destined for Italy, was more than 17 tons.

OPINION

The International Criminal Police Organization, Interpol, defines organized crime thus: "Any group having a corporate structure whose primary objective is to obtain money through illegal activities, often surviving on fear and corruption."

THE MAFIA

The most infamous group of organized criminals in this century is the Mafia. Originally from Sicily and still operating there, they are a loosely connected family-based association of criminal groups that have existed for hundreds of years.

Around the turn of the century, several Mafia members emigrated to America, where they quickly reestablished criminal groups and networks. At first, their activities were confined to extortion and protection rackets, but in 1920, Prohibition provided them with a lucrative, but illegal, trading commodity—alcohol.

Legendary American gangster Al Capone

PROHIBITION

Although the introduction of Prohibition in the United States made alcohol illegal, organized crime made it profitable. Prohibition was introduced to counter what many saw as a growing wave of lawless behavior caused by drunkenness. But Prohibition created its own crime wave. Between the years of 1920 and 1933, 500,000 people were sent to prison for offenses against the Volstead Act, the legislation that had brought about Prohibition.

Much of this crime was associated with the Mafia, or Mob. As well as "rum-running" (smuggling alcohol), the Mob ran illegal nightclubs, known as speakeasies, where "bootleg" liquor was sold. These were frequented by fashionable people and often by local politicians and police officers. There was great rivalry between different gangs. During the thirteen years of Prohibition, nearly 800 mobsters were killed in gangland shoot-outs in Chicago. Prohibition was finally abandoned in December 1933, when it was acknowledged that it was totally unenforceable.

Federal agents pour away twenty barrels of illegal beer in New Jersey, July 1930.

OPINION

"...it can be argued that some of America's biggest villains during the Prohibition era were not the Al Capones, Johnny Torrios, Gus Morans, Dutch Schultzes, or Frank Costellos but the political bosses in New York, Chicago, and elsewhere, who used the underworld to their considerable advantage and the many venal, conniving police and law enforcement officials who supplemented their incomes with mobster money."
Edward Behr, *Prohibition*, 1997

KEY MOMENT

Medellin cartels

In December 1991, Pablo Escobar, head of the Medellin cocaine cartel and one of the most powerful drug barons, was killed by government security forces when a gunfight broke out after they had attempted to capture him. Many saw this as the first opportunity to break the power of the cartels.

THE RISE OF DRUG TRAFFICKING

When Prohibition ended, the American Mafia turned from trading in bootleg liquor that, together with loan-sharking, gambling and prostitution, formed the nucleus of its activities, to dealing in drugs. Drug trafficking brought the Mafia into direct competition with other organized crime syndicates, most notably the Chinese triad gangs who had been running opium dens in the United States for many years. Since the 1930s, the smuggling of, and trading in, illegal drugs has mushroomed to become the major focus for the activities of much organized crime.

An opium den in New York City's Chinatown in 1926

In Colombia since the late 1970s, "drug barons" have run associations of gangs known as cartels. Many of these men have become so fabulously wealthy and powerful that the authorities have great difficulty in bringing them to justice. In 1984, the Colombian government launched a crackdown on the cocaine cartels, but the gangs merely joined forces and became even stronger. Some progress was made in the early 1990s when drug traffickers were offered an amnesty. But most of the violence in Colombia, which is one of the most violent countries in the world, is drug-related. Similarly, the high murder rate in Jamaica, which many drug traffickers use as a base for smuggling cocaine, is linked to drug gangs competing for territory.

Since the collapse of the former Soviet Union, there has been a tremendous growth in the activities of Mafia-style gangs in Russia. Such gangs were responsible for a 25 percent increase in the crime rate in 1992. They have established links with other organized crime groups in other countries. The increasing ease of travel around Europe has attracted gangs in Eastern Europe to traffic in drugs such as heroin and marijuana from Pakistan and Afghanistan en route to Great Britain. These gangs also traffic in illegal immigrants, enticing poverty-stricken people with promises of jobs and a new life. Young women are smuggled into Austria, Italy, the Netherlands, Germany, Scandinavia, and Denmark, lured with promises of work as dancers only to find they are forced, by poverty and their status as illegal immigrants, into prostitution.

Today, organized crime thrives on the ease of access to international markets for drugs and connections with similar groups in other countries. Members of international gangs find hideouts in countries that cannot afford to police incomers adequately or that do not enforce international treaties on extradition. Today there is a great need for international co-operation to combat the activities of powerful organized criminal gangs.

OPINION

At the World Ministerial Conference on Organized Transnational Crime in Naples, Italy, on November 22, 1994, the then UN secretary-general Boutros Boutros-Ghali said: "Organized crime has thus become a world phenomenon. In Europe, in Asia, in Africa, and in America, the forces of darkness are at work and no society is spared." He went on to say: "Transnational crime undermines the very foundations of the international democratic order. Transnational crime poisons the business climate, corrupts political leaders and undermines human rights."

A surprise police raid on a makeshift cocaine-processing laboratory in Bolivia, one of the efforts to combat drug cartels in South America

POLITICAL CRIMES

OPINION

When Chiang Ching, the widow of Mao Zedong, founder and chairman of the People's Republic of China, was convicted of counterrevolutionary activities on January 25, 1981, she said: "Making revolution is no crime."

A large proportion of crime is against people or property, for monetary gain. But people also commit crimes because their beliefs conflict with the policy of a government or of those in positions of power. Occasionally, otherwise law-abiding people are prepared to break the law and risk the penalties because they believe that certain policies are wrong and need to be changed. This chapter looks at some of the groups and individuals who have broken the law to "fight the system."

Militant suffragettes attract attention to their cause by smashing windows in London's Oxford Street in 1912.

Depending on one's viewpoint, breaking the law for political ends may be either the action of a "freedom fighter" or a "terrorist." A freedom fighter is someone who rebels against an unjust or oppressive government in power or against the civil authorities. A terrorist uses unwarranted violence—murder, kidnapping, bombings—to achieve a political purpose. Terrorists often use violence against the civilian population in order to affect government policy. Despite loose and often unjustified attachment of the terrorist label to revolutionaries in civil conflicts, not all orchestrated domestic political violence is terrorism. International law regards irregular warfare waged by revolutionaries against military targets as distinct from the deliberate killing of civilians, indiscriminate bombings of nonmilitary targets, and violence or threats of violence against the population at large.

FREEDOM TO VOTE

Some might argue that the early campaigners for women's rights were freedom fighters; others might say they were terrorists. In Britain in 1903, Emmeline Pankhurst formed the Women's Social and Political Union. She and her followers began a militant campaign to win the right for women to vote. Their campaign involved disruption and vandalism, often with the express purpose of getting arrested, to draw attention to their demands. In 1907, suffragettes stormed the British parliament; they stopped traffic, broke windows, and some even threw themselves in front of politicians' cars. Their actions, though disapproved of by many, gave the cause high-profile status. However, although they included acts of vandalism, the activities of the suffragettes were not intended to harm the civilian population.

In democratic countries it is not a crime for people to demonstrate against policies with which they do not agree. However, this activity becomes illegal when the "public peace" is disturbed and demonstrators use force and violence. The demonstration then becomes a riot. Throughout the century, people have rioted for a wide variety of political reasons, for example: against racial discrimination, foreign rule, oppressive government policies, prison conditions, and unfair taxes.

KEY MOMENT

The Soweto uprising
In South Africa, on June 19, 1976, violence broke out in the Soweto township on the outskirts of Johannesburg. A group of young black people had assembled to protest against the government order to teach black children Afrikaans (the language of the then ruling white minority) in schools. The police fired tear gas into the crowd. The protestors responded by throwing stones. The police then opened fire, killing and injuring a number of children. The Soweto incident inflamed the black people of the South African townships, and days of rioting followed.

In 1968, France was brought to a standstill when students and workers rioted in protest at both the Vietnam War and the French education system.

TERRORISM

In the nineteenth century, terrorist tactics were used by anarchistic groups in Italy, Spain, and France. Since the 1920s, the Irish Republican army has actively opposed the connection of Northern Ireland to Great Britain and sustained a guerrilla war against British forces in support of Irish independence. However, it was not until the 1960s that serious international terrorism developed.

Attacks on civilians by terrorists are not a feature just of the late twentieth century. Here a Spanish anarchist's bomb explodes in the Liceo theater in Barcelona in 1893.

Until that time, terrorist activities were conducted mainly by indigenous groups fighting colonial rule. In India in the 1930s, Hindus rose up against the British occupation, as did the Mau-Mau in Kenya in the 1950s. During the 1940s, the Zionist Stern Gang used bombing and assassination against both the British and the Arabs in their struggle for an independent Israel; and the FLN, National Liberation Front, used violence in their fight against French rule in Algeria.

However, the 1960s saw the growth of left-wing terrorism that aimed to bring down the state. In West Germany, the Red Army Faction, otherwise known as the Baader-Meinhoff Gang, conducted bank robberies and raided American military bases. In 1977, they kidnapped the industrialist Hans-Martin Schleyer and eventually murdered him. But by the end of the 1970s, having failed in their goal, most of the gang were either dead or in prison.

Le Petit Journal

TOUS LES JOURS
Le Petit Journal
5 Centimes

SUPPLÉMENT ILLUSTRÉ
Hult pages : CINQ centimes

TOUS LES VENDREDIS
Le Supplément Illustré
5 Centimes

Quatrième Année   SAMEDI 25 NOVEMBRE 1893   Numéro 157

LA DYNAMITE EN ESPAGNE
Explosion d'une bombe au théâtre du Liceo à Barcelone

The conflict between Israel and the Arab nations has accounted for a large proportion of the terrorism carried out during the second half of the twentieth century. In 1972, a group of Palestinian Arabs known as the Black September group took hostage and subsequently murdered eleven Israeli athletes at the Munich Olympic games. This action was followed by a wave of aircraft and airport bombings. In the 1990s incidents such as the garage bombing of the World Trade Center in New York City, the attack against western tourists in Egypt and, in 1998, the bombing of the American embassy in Nairobi, Kenya, can be related to the rise of Islamic fundamentalism and anti-American feeling. These sentiments stem partly from continued American support for Israel and its military presence in Arab countries.

Several "ex-terrorist" leaders have gone on to head governments set up as a result of their political activities. In Cuba, Communists led by Fidel Castro overthrew the government of dictator Fulgencio Batista in 1959. Castro has been prime minister of Cuba since that date. Yasser Arafat, the leader of the Palestinian Liberation Organization, went on to become head of the Arab delegation in the peace talks with Israel. And Nelson Mandela, who was sentenced in 1964 to life imprisonment for treason and was accused of being a terrorist at his trial, became president of South Africa in 1994.

> ### KEY MOMENT
>
> **Lockerbie**
> On December 22, 1988, Pan American Flight 103 was destroyed by a terrorist bomb over the small Scottish town of Lockerbie. The jumbo jet crashed, killing 259 people on board and eleven on the ground. Various American embassies had received prior warnings that a Pan Am flight would be a terrorist bomb target. In 1991, two Libyan intelligence officers were accused of planting the bomb. In 1992, the United Nations imposed sanctions on Libya after the country refused to hand over the two men, for trial. In December 1998, Libya eventually agreed that the men should face trial in the Netherlands.

Egyptian security officers stand by the remains of a tourist bus. Nine people were killed and another nine injured when a bomb exploded on the bus in September 1997.

ASSASSINATIONS

Whether political assassination is a terrorist act depends on its association with a broader program of political violence. Thus the assassinations of U.S. presidents Abraham Lincoln, William McKinley, and John F. Kennedy, although undoubtedly politically motivated, cannot properly be called terrorism. On the other hand, the assassinations of Czar Alexander II of Russia, of Salvador Allende of Chile (killed during a military coup in 1973), of Indian prime minister Indira Gandhi (shot by one of her Sikh security guards in 1984), and of her son (killed by an assassin's bomb in 1991) were part of concerted programs of political violence and, therefore, fit the terrorism definition.

ESPIONAGE

Espionage is the practice of spying to acquire information. It involves conveying secret information to an intelligence agency for evaluation. Espionage is an important source of information for any government attempting to learn the secrets of other nations.

In 1917, the female spy Mata Hari was shot by a French firing squad for espionage activities. Born in the Netherlands, Mata Hari was a captivating dancer who had many affairs with French military officers. She was accused of joining the German secret service in 1907 and of passing on to them French military secrets confided to her by her lovers.

The spy Mata Hari, whose real name was Gertrud Zelle, performing one of her exotic dances.

Espionage activities are punished most severely if one is spying against one's own country. At this point, the spy's crime becomes one of treason. In the United States during the 1950s, Julius and Ethel Rosenberg were accused of leading a network of spies and gleaning secrets about the atom bomb, which they sold to the Russians. Their case epitomizes the wave of anti-Communist feeling that was sweeping the West at this time—a period sometimes referred to as "the Great Red Scare." The Rosenbergs were executed on June 19, 1953. But many people believed that they were the innocent victims of Cold War hysteria.

Four-year-old Michael and six-year-old Robert Rosenberg read of their parents' imminent death in a newspaper. Julius and Ethel Rosenberg (pictured left) were executed the following day.

Meanwhile, in the UK, Foreign Office civil servants Guy Burgess and Donald Mclean disappeared in 1951. Six months later they sent a telegram saying that they were "taking a long Mediterranean holiday," although by this time most people believed that they had been spying for the Soviet Union and had fled there. These suspicions were confirmed in 1956, when Burgess and Mclean issued a statement saying that they had gone to live in the Soviet Union to work for better understanding between that nation and the West.

As the century has progressed, political crimes have been played out on an increasingly international stage. The principal obstacles to dealing with crimes such as terrorism and espionage arise from their international dimensions. Whereas domestic terrorism is the responsibility of local law-enforcement authorities, international terrorism is often beyond the reach of national criminal law and jurisdiction.

KEY MOMENT

The hanging of Roger Casement

On August 3, 1916, Sir Roger Casement was hanged for high treason in London. An Irish nationalist and revolutionary, he was accused and convicted of smuggling arms to Ireland to help the fight for independence. Casement may have been executed to deter other revolutionaries, but he came to be seen as a martyr for the Irish cause, and his death fueled anti-English feeling.

POLICING

The police are responsible for maintaining public order, for protecting people from unlawful acts, and for detecting and preventing crime. Many ideas the public has about police work come from television programs and movies, but these portrayals are often not very accurate.

EARLY LAW ENFORCEMENT AGENTS

Police forces and police departments have developed fairly recently in Western society, dating back no more than 180 years. In the English-speaking world (and beyond), police practices are based on British models. As the British began to colonize North America during the seventeenth century, the colonists adopted the British criminal justice system. During the seventeenth and eighteenth centuries, colonial North America relied on sheriffs, constables, night-watchmen, and security guards for public protection. Appointed by the governor of the colony, the sheriff was the most important law enforcement officer in the county. He was responsible for tax collection, law enforcement, and the maintenance of public facilities. The constable had similar responsibilities but was employed to patrol towns and cities. Night-watchmen were responsible for protecting the city from fires, crime, and suspicious persons.

A suspect is discovered by two London Metropolitan police officers using the new "Nab" light, a battery-operated flashlight, in 1873.

By the early nineteenth century, the law enforcement system could no longer control the crime and disorder that had begun to appear in the cities. As a result, new police forces were established. The London Metropolitan police force was one of the first of its kind in the world. It was set up in 1829 by the British home secretary, Sir Robert Peel, and became a model for policing in all modern industrialized nations. The new police officers differed from the old law-enforcement officials in that they worked both day and night, wore uniforms, and patrolled the streets in an attempt to prevent crime and maintain order. In North America, police officers carried firearms.

During the twentieth century, police efficiency in the West has improved, with better selection of police officers and more technology for aiding crime prevention. Unlike the United States, European countries and Canada and Japan have highly centralized police forces. Great Britain, for example, has some fifty police forces, compared with around 20,000 in the United States. The London Metropolitan Police Service, with its headquarters in Scotland Yard, is the largest force in the country. In France, the Police Nationale is responsible for law enforcement in cities with a population of 10,000 or more. The Gendarmerie Nationale polices the military as well as civilians in towns with fewer than 10,000 inhabitants.

> **KEY MOMENT**
>
> **The Mounties**
> In 1873, the Northwest Mounted Police was created to police on horseback the vast western plains of the Northwest Territories of Canada (present-day Manitoba, Saskatchewan, and Alberta). In 1920 the force was renamed the Royal Canadian Mounted Police (RCMP) and assumed the federal policing of all Canada. Members of the RCMP also enforce laws in provinces (areas) that do not have state police. Over the years the RCMP, nicknamed the "Mounties," has acquired a reputation for persistence and bravery.

Increased surveillance in city centers has reduced crime rates significantly. Two police officers patrol a pedestrian shopping area in Auckland, New Zealand.

The FBI

The Federal Bureau of Investigation (FBI) is the largest and most important law-enforcement organization in the United States today. With more than 8,000 special agents scattered across the country in both large cities and small towns, or based at headquarters in Washington, DC, the FBI is responsible for enforcing hundreds of federal criminal laws. Its cases include kidnappings and bank robberies, efforts to locate fugitives, and analyses of fraud against the government. It also deals with counterintelligence matters (finding and arresting foreign spies working in the United States).

The FBI was created in 1908 by Attorney General Charles Bonaparte. Known originally as the Bureau of Investigation of the Justice Department, it acquired its current name in 1935. One of the first major tasks of the FBI was to enforce the Mann Act (White Slave Act) in 1910. This made it illegal to transport women over state lines for immoral purposes. Over the next few years, the number of FBI special agents grew to more than three hundred. During World War I, the FBI gained responsibility for espionage and sabotage and investigating enemy aliens.

Before computers were used to do the job, fingerprints had to be stored in filing cabinets and matched manually. In vast FBI halls, a million fingerprints a year were filed.

FBI director J. Edgar Hoover (left) studies a report following the arrest of seventeen top Communist party officials in New York and Pittsburgh, during the time of the "Red Scare" in the early 1950s.

The FBI was reorganized in 1924 when J. Edgar Hoover became director. Under Hoover's efficient directorship, new agents were given special training and a national center for criminal records was established. J. Edgar Hoover remained as director of the bureau for forty-eight years and was known as America's "number one cop;" but he was a controversial figure. His death in 1972 was followed by the revelation of a series of abuses of power that had taken place during his tenure. An obituary in *The New York Times* stated: "For nearly a half century, J. Edgar Hoover and the FBI were indistinguishable. That was at once his strength and its weakness...."

Hoover's supporters claimed that he turned the FBI into one of the world's most effective and formidable law-enforcement organizations. But his critics emphasized his anti-Communist, racist views and his rigid, traditional stance. Through the FBI he amassed secret files full of illegally obtained information on many citizens whom he suspected of being Communists. One of these was Dr. Martin Luther King, Jr., whom Hoover called "the most notorious liar in the country."

OPINION

"Pick a small boy these days and ask him who of all the people in the world he wants to be like, and ten to one he will reply—J. Edgar Hoover."
From the *New York World-Telegram*, 1936

DEVELOPMENTS IN DETECTION

In the early days of the century, often the only way of catching a criminal was "red-handed," in the act of committing the crime. The introduction of gas lighting on city streets in the early 1900s was seen as a major step toward reducing crime. The police had few techniques to help them, although they were beginning to use fingerprints, a system developed in Bengal, India, in the 1890s by Sir Edward Henry, the colonial Inspector General of Police. Until computers began to be used in the 1970s, however, detectives had to trawl through hundreds of records to match fingerprints. Today computers can perform the same task in seconds.

Advances have also been made in the identification of criminals by witnesses. In the early days of the century, an artist was employed to draw a likeness of the suspect from a description given by a witness. The portrait would then be circulated. By the late 1930s, these portraits were put together with the help of photographic libraries of facial features. By the 1990s, computers were used to generate these images, which could be sent around the world instantaneously.

Fingerprints are left on a surface because of the oiliness of the skin. When dusted with powder, the print is revealed.

By the end of the twentieth century, advanced technology has enabled enforcement agencies to follow and record our every move. Closed-circuit television (CCTV) is helping reduce crime levels dramatically in city centers. However, some argue that surveillance operations have a serious impact on people's civil liberties and right to privacy.

FORENSICS

It is virtually impossible for someone to commit a crime without leaving behind some clue or trace of themselves. Developments in forensic science have enabled pathologists to pinpoint the exact time and cause of death in all but a few murder cases. Psychologists can build up character profiles of criminals, which give detectives vital leads. People can also be identified from the way they speak. Computers are used routinely to put together databases on known suspects, which are shared between police forces. Sophisticated types of equipment, including aerial observations from helicopters and long-range listening devices, are used for surveillance operations.

One major advance in forensic science has been deoxyribonucleic acid (DNA) profiling. This was invented by the British geneticist Alec Jeffreys and first became available in 1988. DNA profiling is based on the scientific fact that each person has his or her own unique genetic code, which can be easily identified in a small flake of skin, a drop of blood, or a drop of body fluid. As long as suitable evidence has been kept, DNA testing can be used to check the guilt or innocence of people convicted of crimes committed years ago. It is particularly useful for establishing the guilt or innocence of rapists and murderers and has already been responsible for clearing more than 2,000 suspects worldwide, most before they were tried and convicted.

Although new technology offers the detective many new ways of finding and catching criminals, it is also available to the criminals. Thus a constant battle has developed between detective and criminal, both of whom want to stay ahead of the game.

> ## KEY MOMENT
>
> ### Interpol
> The International Criminal Police Organization, or Interpol, was originally established in Vienna in 1923, and reconstituted in Paris after World War II. Interpol exchanges information among its police members about criminals who operate in more than one country, whose crimes affect other countries, or who have fled from one country to another to escape prosecution. It has an international criminal register, fingerprint files, and various criminal databases that allow an exchange of information on drug traffickers, terrorists, and organized crime. Interpol has 177 member states.

To obtain a fingerprint, the end of each finger is inked and then pressed onto a surface.

IN THE FIRING LINE

Throughout the century, police forces around the world have faced allegations that they have acted unfairly, fabricated evidence to secure convictions, or used unacceptable methods to extract confessions from suspects. In Great Britain in 1929, a Royal Commission on police powers expressed concern that confessions "seemed not always to have been given voluntarily," implying undue pressure from the police. During Prohibition in the United States, the bribing of police officers was rife, and for many years, there have been allegations that the Mafia has infiltrated and exerted a strong influence within U.S. police organizations. Several miscarriages of justice have taken place in which the police have withheld evidence or lied to get a conviction. In England, the "Guildford Four" were four men who spent many years in prison, having been accused of bombing a pub in Guildford. Their conviction was finally quashed, and they were acquitted. After their release, the Lord Chief Justice said that the Surrey police "must have lied" at the trial.

Brian Conlon, one of the "Guildford Four," waves to supporters after his release from prison in October 1989. The Guildford Four were acquitted after spending fifteen years in prison in England.

KEY MOMENT

Police casualty
On February 20, 1991, Catherine Choutron became the first female police officer to be killed in France since women were admitted to the force in 1975. She was shot by a gunman driving a stolen car.

Commenting on the high level of corruption in the London Metropolitan Police during the 1970s, the then commissioner, Sir Robert Mark, said that the force should catch more criminals than it employed. Although action was taken to "clean-up the Met" it is thought that by the late 1990s, there are still a significant number of corrupt detectives in the force.

Police have also been accused of not doing enough. In Belgium in 1996, a report found that police officers had been grossly negligent in their efforts to apprehend Marc Dutroux, a suspect in a child-sex ring. Despite a number of clues and tip-offs and, at one point, a search of his home, they failed to find two eight-year-old girls held prisoner in his basement. The Belgian public were horrified. The case sparked off a national outrage against pedophilia and the police. As a result, Belgium's interior and justice ministers resigned in April 1998.

REFLECTING SOCIETY

During the century, though Western society has become more multiracial, and women have played an increasing role outside the home, police forces have by and large failed to reflect these changes. It has been difficult for the police to defend themselves against accusations of racism and sexism in their recruiting policies when groups such as women and black people remain underrepresented within the force. In the latter years of the century, more positive measures have been taken to ensure that the structure of the police force reflects more accurately the society it represents, though problems still remain.

In many respects, as the century has progressed, the role of the police has become an unenviable one. Hundreds of police officers have been injured or killed in the line of duty. Their job has become increasingly difficult as criminals use more sophisticated means, and the public demands greater accountability and performance. But the maintenance of law and order is fundamental to democracy, and efficient, honest, and fair policing is an important part of this.

> **KEY MOMENT**
>
> **The murder of Stephen Lawrence**
> The case of Stephen Lawrence, an 18-year-old black youth stabbed to death at a bus stop in south London in April 1993, has had an important impact on the policing of Britain. An inquiry into the case suggested that Lawrence's killers went free because of police incompetence and lack of interest because the victim was black. Thanks to the efforts of Lawrence's parents, the case received enormous publicity and has led to an examination of racism within the police force.

In some cases, police officers need to be armed for their own safety. This Russian special officer wears a mask to hide his identity while arresting a suspect on drug-related charges in Moscow in 1997.

THE JUDICIAL SYSTEM

A lawyer addresses jurors in a mock court room in Moscow. After the collapse of Communism in the late 1980s, Russia's legal system changed to involve trial by jury.

The criminal justice system of a country enacts the laws governing social behavior, attempts to prevent violations of the law and apprehends, judges, and punishes those who violate them. The judicial system determines how the laws are administered; this is usually achieved through the courts, where trials and hearings take place. Judicial systems vary from country to country and are the product of centuries of history. In Western societies the foundations for an independent judiciary were laid during the Reformation in the sixteenth century and the French Revolution toward the end of the eighteenth century. During this time, the power of the state and the involvement of the Church in the judicial system came to be challenged. This power continued to diminish during the twentieth century, as the independence of the judiciary came to be considered of paramount importance.

Means of apprehending criminals vary throughout the world. Here photographs and descriptions of suspected criminals are publicly displayed in China as part of a drive against crime.

NATIONAL DIFFERENCES

Elsewhere in the world, the independence of judicial systems has been continually challenged by political and religious dogma throughout the century. During the 1930s, the revolutionary courts of the USSR under Josef Stalin were used to further the leader's own purposes. Following the assassination of Sergei Kirov in 1934, a member of the Politburo (the chief committee of the USSR Communist Party), "show trials" were used to try more than a hundred of Stalin's rivals. They were summarily found guilty and executed.

The Chinese have a tradition of judicial process that differs considerably from that of Western nations. Historically, law and order has been the responsibility of the family or the local community. Since 1978 efforts have been made to bring the judicial and legal system more into line with Western models, and in 1982 the right to a legal defense was introduced. Despite this, the state still controls the judiciary and the right to a legal defense is not enforced or respected. Those who criticize the government are imprisoned for "counter-revolutionary" crimes or, more recently, "endangering state security." Such trials are often highly publicized as an example to the Chinese public.

KEY MOMENT

The Dreyfus case
In France at the beginning of the twentieth century, the case of Alfred Dreyfus highlighted the importance of the independence of the judicial system. Dreyfus, a Jewish army officer in the French military, was twice court-martialed and wrongly convicted of spying for Germany. His conviction was the direct result of anti-Jewish feeling in the French Army and the Catholic Church. The injustice of the treatment he received caused an enormous outcry in France. It was a significant factor in the election of a more liberal government, which brought in legislation to separate church and state, and thereby the judiciary, in 1905. On September 19, 1900, Dreyfus was pardoned by the president of France.

KEY MOMENT

Miranda v. Arizona

In 1966 the Miranda ruling was made by the U.S. Supreme Court. Ernesto Miranda had been arrested for the rape of a woman in Arizona. He was identified by the victim and questioned for two hours; he then made a confession to the authorities. However, he was never told that he had the right to remain silent and to have a lawyer present at his questioning. His confession was presented as evidence, and he was convicted. Miranda appealed to the Supreme Court, which ruled that incriminating statements such as confessions were inadmissible if the defendants had not already been informed of their right to remain silent. This decision was considered a landmark in American civil liberties, although others suggest that it has seriously hampered the ability of the police to solve serious crimes.

THE SHARI'A

In many Muslim countries the second half of the twentieth century has seen the growing power of Islamic religious law—the Shari'a. This is the sacred law of Islam. Countries that have totally, or partially, adopted this as the law of the land include Saudi Arabia, Pakistan, and Afghanistan. Strictly interpreted, Shari'a law provides for the punishment of adulterers by stoning and imposes the death penalty on those who commit the crime of "apostasy" —the abandonment of the Muslim faith. However, many argue that although these laws are carried out under the name of Islam, this type of punishment is denounced in the Koran—the holy book of Islam. There are claims that governments are using these laws to suppress women and government critics. Other Muslim countries that have adopted the Shari'a law interpret it less harshly.

Under arrest: Pietro Aglieri, one of Italy's most-wanted Mafia godfathers, is led in handcuffs out of a police station in Palermo, Sicily, in June 1997.

The acquittal of four white police officers accused of the beating of Rodney King unleashed long-felt resentments in the black community in Los Angeles and resulted in days of rioting.

ARREST PROCEDURES

In Great Britain and the United States, when police officers have probable cause to believe that a person has violated a law, they are legally empowered to make an arrest. People who have been arrested are read their rights and then charged or later summoned to appear before the court. Some of those who are charged are kept in police custody or else remanded in custody (held in prison) before they appear in court. When the suspect appears in court, the charges are formally filed with the court and read to the defendant. Defendants are provided with legal representation if they do not have it already, and a plea is entered. With a plea of guilty, the defendant waives the right to a trial and may be sentenced by a judge or magistrate immediately. If the defendant pleads not guilty, he or she may be tried then and there, or else a trial date at a higher court is set.

> ### KEY MOMENT
>
> **The Rodney King case**
> In April 1992, four Los Angeles police officers were acquitted by a jury of twelve white people of beating a black motorist, Rodney King. An amateur videotape of the incident showed men in police officers' uniforms beating and kicking King. The trial verdict sparked off the worst rioting in modern American history. People felt the case made clear the racism of the Los Angeles police force and the injustice of the legal process, in particular a biased jury. The riots left fifty-five people dead.

In most English-speaking countries, the evidence is put before a jury made up of members of the public who decide on the innocence or guilt of the defendant. Uniquely in Scotland, a jury is able to return a verdict of "not-proven" (as well as one of guilty/not guilty). Many believe that the right to be tried by one's peers is a fundamental right. But there have been occasions during the century when this right has not served the defendants or justice well: juries have been accused of being biased, prejudiced, or unable to understand and follow the court procedures.

In the countries of continental Europe, whose legal systems are based on European civil law, responsibility for case investigations usually rests with the judge. With the assistance of the suspect, the judge clarifies disputed facts and plays a key role in deciding whether a case should be prosecuted. Trials are held before a judicial tribunal. Trial by jury is no longer practiced in Germany, France, or the Netherlands.

A FAIR TRIAL?

In the United States during the 1930s the Scottsboro boys, nine black youths, were tried and found guilty of

The Scottsboro boys conferring with their lawyer, Sam Leibowitz, in 1933

raping two white women in the state of Tennessee. At this time institutionalized racism was widespread in many parts of the United States. No black people were allowed to serve on the jury that tried the Scottsboro boys. After the trial, the two women retracted their accusations, and their convictions were set aside by the Supreme Court on appeal. But at a retrial the nine youths were still found guilty by another white jury and were forced to continue with their prison sentences. They almost certainly did not commit the crime of which they were accused.

The jubilant Maxwell brothers, Ian (left) and Kevin, after their trial in 1996

Trials involving cases of fraud and embezzlement are complex and hard to follow. Today it is argued that there should be an "expert panel" to try these cases rather than a jury made up of the general public. In the UK in 1996 the trial of the Maxwell brothers was a case in point. Ian and Kevin Maxwell, sons of media mogul Robert Maxwell, were charged with conspiring to commit fraud relating to the pension funds of the private Maxwell companies. The evidence was highly technical and complicated. The brothers were eventually cleared of all charges, following an eight-month trial that cost British taxpayers $30 million.

The Louise Woodward case

While working in the United States, British nanny Louise Woodward was accused of killing twenty-one-month-old Matthew Eappen when he was left in her care. The verdict of murder was later reduced to manslaughter. Speaking about her experience of being the first Englishwoman to be tried on live television, Woodward said: "I would hate [in Great Britain] to see it go the way it has in the U.S....These are people's lives you're dealing with—this is not a soap opera ... do you really want the public to be policing the courtroom and making those decisions instead of the twelve people? You may as well have an opinion poll on TV."

JUSTICE AND THE MEDIA

During the twentieth century, the media (first newspapers and later television and the Internet) have rushed to bring news of the latest crimes and court cases to the attention of the public. However, earlier in the century, judgments made one day were brought to people in the first editions of the next day's newspapers. Today they can be released instantaneously on the Internet. And though the media compulsion to satisfy the public's appetite for news of crime is not restricted to the last decades of the century, it is increasingly jeopardizing both the rights of the defendants and the likelihood of securing convictions. This seems particularly to be the case where celebrities are involved.

In 1927, Charles Lindbergh was the first man to fly across the Atlantic alone, an accomplishment that drew much media attention to himself and his wife. In 1934 their baby son was kidnapped and later found dead. The newspaper coverage of the case urged the police to catch someone for the crime and secure a conviction. A German immigrant was convicted of the baby's murder and then executed, but his guilt is still in doubt today.

Louise Woodward pleading her innocence during her sentencing hearing before American judge Hiller Zobel in November 1997

Controversial cases are bound to receive much pretrial publicity. This makes it difficult to ensure that jurors have not already formed an opinion about the case. This problem arose during the O. J. Simpson case, when the celebrity was accused of killing his former wife, Nicole Brown Simpson, and her friend Ron Goldman in 1995. O. J. Simpson was a famous football player and movie star. After a nine-month trial, Simpson was found not guilty amid much controversy.

Some countries have introduced the televising of court cases. On one hand, this satisfies people who argue that the public has the right to know what goes on in a court room; on the other, it may have an effect on the way people behave in court and on the decision that the jury eventually arrives at. In America, during the trial of Dr. Samuel Sheppard in 1955, proceedings were disrupted by cameras, and witnesses were harassed by reporters while testifying. As a result of the chaos, Dr. Sheppard's conviction was reversed by the Supreme Court.

Dr. Sam Sheppard (center) walking through the gates of the Ohio Penitentiary on July 20, 1955, about to begin a life sentence for killing his wife. Sheppard's conviction was subsequently reversed by the Supreme Court.

During the twentieth century, the public's confidence in the ability of our institutions to deliver justice has been seriously eroded. The innocent have been convicted because evidence has been suppressed; the rich have often received preferential treatment; and the cumbersome nature of the justice system has occasionally allowed the guilty to go free.

PUNISHMENT AND PRISON

Throughout history, there have been wide-ranging ideas about the best ways to deal with criminals. The argument essentially comes down to the distinction between retribution (punishment) and reform. Retribution is based on religious doctrine; it is the act of punishing wrongdoers for the evil they have done. Reform, on the other hand, means to improve by correcting bad patterns of behavior. Reformers take into account the particular circumstances of offenders and help them make adjustments to their behavior so that they can fit back into society.

Until the eighteenth century, retribution was the prime motivation for punishment, and criminals were treated extremely severely. Exile, execution, and various forms of corporal (physical) punishment, such as public flogging and beating, were the most common penalties for criminal acts. Prisons were originally used as places to hold people before they went to trial. In Europe, during the Enlightenment in the eighteenth century, the extreme harshness of most punishment was questioned for the first time. Attempts were made to fit the severity of the punishment to the severity of the crime. The belief was that fairly administered penalties would deter criminals from reoffending. In this way deterrence, rather than retribution, became a leading principle of the European criminal justice system.

Early in the century, punishment was often harsh and brutal. In 1900 Louise Masset was hanged at Newgate, London, for killing her five-year-old son.

CHILDREN AND CRIME

In the past, child criminals were often treated as adults when it came to punishment, and sentences could be harsh. But by the end of the nineteenth century, there was a general recognition that children needed different treatment. In 1899, the first special court for juveniles was set up in Chicago. Throughout the twentieth century, special measures and facilities for young people have gradually been introduced.

Early in the twentieth century the idea was argued that it would be better to try to prevent crime from taking place at all by tackling the underlying causes of crime. The emphasis, it was argued, should be on fighting the factors that contribute toward crime, such as poverty and lack of education. For most of the century, in Western society, attitudes toward punishment have become less harsh. Many have argued that this approach does not reform criminals or reduce crime. There have been continual calls for punishment to be more severe, and recently the sentencing climate has once again become much tougher.

OPINION

"The defendant of wealth and position never goes to the electric chair or the gallows." Lewis E. Lawes, warden of Sing Sing state prison in Ossining, NY, during the 1920s and 1930s

Elizabeth Fry was a Quaker who was dedicated to reforming conditions in British prisons. Her primary concern was for women and their children in prison. On her visits she discovered no bedding, toilets, heating, ventilation, or light.

KEY MOMENT

The founding of Borstals

In 1902, the first Borstal was founded in a village of the same name in Kent in England. Thereafter, Borstals sprang up throughout Great Britain. A combination of correctional school and a custodial sentence for adolescents, Borstals relied on a strict training regime. Initially, they were seen as a success because there was little recidivism among those who had attended them. However, their effectiveness decreased, and in the 1970s they were replaced by youth custody centers and, subsequently, by young offender institutions.

Young men line up at a Borstal institution in Middlesex, England, probably in the early 1950s.

VARIOUS METHODS OF PUNISHMENT

The punishment someone convicted of a crime can expect varies enormously, depending on the severity of the crime committed. Corporal punishment was common in the first half of the twentieth century but was phased out in Great Britain and eventually outlawed by the Criminal Justice Act of 1948. It is now rare in the Western world but has increased, in the form of stonings and beatings, in some Islamic countries that have strictly adopted the Shari'a law. For more serious crimes, imprisonment is the usual form of punishment, but fines have become the main penalty for less serious offenses.

Gradually, the well-ordered, physically isolated prison came to be seen as the best way of instilling discipline, removing temptation, and rehabilitating the offender. By 1900, prisons were firmly established in most Western countries as the main means of punishing people for serious crimes. The most familiar image of a prison is a large, fortresslike building, such as the maximum security San Quentin Prison in California. But there are also medium- and minimum-security prisons today. These are identified by their openness and lack of strict security procedures. People held in the latter are judged to be less dangerous than those incarcerated in maximum security institutions.

Today, as a result of the large numbers of prisoners, overcrowding is commonplace. This can lead to higher levels of tension and aggression and contributes to prison riots. Prisons have constantly been the focus of debate concerning their appropriateness for all types of criminals. In particular, it has been suggested that the prison system is an unsuitable method for dealing with juvenile offenders. This unsuitability, combined with the increasing costs of keeping people in prison, has led to alternative ways of curbing the criminal activities of nonviolent offenders. In some cases, a small, non-removable electronic tag is attached to the criminal; this allows the police to monitor his or her whereabouts at all times.

NONCUSTODIAL SENTENCES

During the 1960s, society began to adopt a more liberal approach to punishment, and noncustodial sentences were introduced. In some cases, where appropriate, convicted criminals were put on probation and sentenced to community service. In 1968, the British Parole Board was created. This system enabled prisoners to gain early release from prison on condition that they report to a designated officer and agree to undergo a program of rehabilitation. Following the Scandinavian model, open prisons were built where prisoners had more freedom and in some cases could go out to work during the day.

The criminal justice system in Sweden contrasts with those elsewhere in the world. Here the belief is that only truly dangerous criminals should be incarcerated. Sweden, therefore, offers alternatives, such as fines, to prison. If criminals are sent to prison, they are offered facilities such as psychiatric treatment and a university release program. However, recent evidence suggests that Sweden, like many other countries in the West, suffers from a high rate of recidivism (re-offending), and attitudes in favor of more severe forms of punishment may be hardening.

OPINION

"People should not be sent to prison if there are other acceptable ways of dealing with them."
Lord Taylor of Gosforth, England, in an interview in *The Times* newspaper, 1994

A prisoner released on parole in Ohio is fitted with an electronic ankle tag so that the authorities can keep track of his whereabouts.

In September 1989, new participants in the Sumter County Correctional Institution "Boot Camp" program arrive at their barracks.

In the 1980 and 1990s, criticism began to be voiced about liberal forms of punishment. A backlash against the "soft" approach to criminal behavior was expressed through the government policies of President Ronald Reagan and British Prime Minister Margaret Thatcher. Media attention was drawn to recreational programs for young offenders; such programs were perceived, unfairly, as a way of simply giving bad kids a vacation at the taxpayers' expense. Public attitudes hardened, and there were demands for longer and harsher sentences for criminals. In the United States, young offenders may now be sentenced to short-term "shock-incarceration units," or boot camps. Here they undergo a rigid, grueling regime of military-type exercises, in the belief that a "short sharp shock" will deter those convicted from reoffending. However, those boot camps that rely solely on tough regimes have not been effective. In Great Britain and in the United States, long prison sentences are now imposed on those convicted of three or more offenses—a policy known as "three strikes and you're out"—even if the crimes committed were relatively minor.

CAPITAL PUNISHMENT

Capital punishment is the legal taking of a life and is the most severe form of punishment. So-called capital crimes, those that carry the possibility of the death penalty, change with time and differ from country to country. But despite its continued support from the general public in most countries, capital punishment has never proved an effective deterrent to murder.

For this reason, and because many consider it to be immoral, capital punishment has been abolished during the twentieth century in all established democracies apart from Japan and the United States. It was abolished in Great Britain in 1965, Canada in 1976, and in most European countries during the 1990s. The U.S. Supreme Court banned capital punishment in 1972, but in 1976 ordered its resumption. Each U.S. state now decides for itself whether or not to have the death penalty. No Arab countries and few African countries have abolished the death penalty. In China, Malaysia, and Iran, capital punishment is used for a wide range of crimes, including drug offenses.

Methods of execution have changed during the century and from country to country. The traditional method throughout the English-speaking world used to be hanging. Military executions took place by firing squad. Electrocution was introduced in New York State in 1890, the gas chamber in Nevada in 1923, and the lethal injection in Oklahoma in 1977. In some Islamic countries beheading and stoning are sometimes practiced as methods of execution.

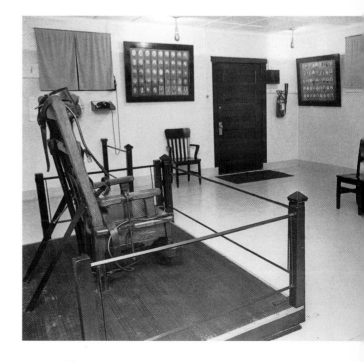

A once popular form of execution: prisoners were strapped into chairs such as this before being electrocuted.

53

PRISON LIFE

Life in prison, although to most people a preferential state to that of death by execution, brings with it many pains and hardships that are perhaps forgotten by those on the outside. The first is the deprivation of liberty and the loneliness and boredom of imprisonment. Second, prisoners are deprived of most goods and services from the outside world. Third, for the majority, is the absence of heterosexual relationships. Fourth, prisoners are subjected to institutional rules designed to control every aspect of their behavior. By and large, all these factors have remained more or less constant throughout the twentieth century.

MEN AND WOMEN IN PRISON

Male and female prison cultures, however, differ fundamentally. The male inmate is thrown into prolonged intimacy with other men and is forced to take an aggressive stance and to be constantly wary for his personal safety. Physical attacks are commonplace. In female prisons there is less violence, by and large, but different groups do come into conflict. Women tend to be held in smaller prisons with fewer programs and recreational opportunities.

Inmates and staff working at the prison radio station of Dade County jail, Miami, Florida

In Great Britain, despite the fact that the female prison population has doubled since the beginning of the 1990s, little has been done to make prisons more suitable for women. Prisons, as institutions, were designed for men, and several incidents in the 1990s have raised questions about their appropriateness for women. Overall, women enter prisons with more serious health problems than men. Mothers may have the burden of concern about the care of their children while they are inside. There are no facilities where women can spend time with their children, and, in some notorious cases, women giving birth in the hospital have been shackled to their beds to prevent their escaping.

Although changes in attitudes and policies have had some impact on the penal system during the twentieth century, it appears that the major instrument of punishment for the most serious crimes will remain the prison. However, in the light of the difficulties surrounding its use, many people think that prison should be used only as a last resort for those offenders who cannot be handled in any other way.

A home for female juvenile offenders in Ryazan, a town south of Moscow, Russia. Politicians such as Vladimir Zhirinovsky, who promise to crush crime, are popular in Russia.

OPINION

"Very few [women prisoners] present a threat, and most respond to even the smallest amount of support—if it's offered. So when will we begin to treat them with some humanity?" Pat Carlen, British criminologist

THE INTERNATIONALIZATION OF CRIME

Although it seems that, at the end of the twentieth century, crime rates are leveling out and in many cases falling, some crimes, particularly large-scale drug trafficking carried out by highly organized criminal groups, and terrorism, continue to present major challenges to law-enforcement agencies around the world.

A Cambodian man ponders the past at one of the many killing fields sites in his country. At least a million people were massacred under the brutal regime of Pol Pot during the late 1970s.

Ease of access to international markets for drugs, more developed transportation systems, the Internet, and other sophisticated forms of technology have all contributed to the internationalization of these crimes. However, at the same time, the international community is becoming more organized and determined to stamp out this kind of crime. It is helped by the co-ordination of criminal records through organizations such as Interpol and the establishment of extradition treaties between countries.

INTERNATIONAL LAW

The twentieth century has seen major developments in international agreements and conventions, many of which are concerned with tackling international crime. In 1945, after the end of World War II, the United Nations was established with an elaborate machinery for settling disputes. The International Court of Justice was set up as the judicial body of the UN. Countries may now refer cases to the Court, but its rulings are not binding. It has no power to enforce the decisions it makes. For instance, in 1980 the Court ordered Iran to release fifty-three American hostages, but the ruling was simply ignored. In 1985, the Court ruled against the United States' planting mines in the harbors of Nicaragua, but the Reagan administration also ignored its ruling. The following year, the United States withdrew its policy of compliance with the Court, thereby substantially weakening its power.

WAR CRIMES AND GENOCIDE

Following World War II, trials in Nuremberg, Germany, brought Nazi leaders to account for their actions during the war. The Nuremberg trials established that, under war conditions, there are three categories of crime: crimes against peace; crimes that violate the Hague Convention, which sets out ground rules for wars; and crimes against humanity, such as the extermination of racial, ethnic, and religious groups. The Nuremberg trials were an important step in the evolution of international penal law. However, a paradox of the twentieth century is that those who murder one person are more likely to be brought to justice than those who plot genocide against millions.

KEY MOMENT

Genocide in Rwanda
On September 2, 1998, Jean-Paul Akayesu was found guilty of genocide. This was the first ever judgment on the crime of genocide to be passed by an international court. Akayesu's crimes related to the massacre of thousands of Tutsis by the Hutu-dominated army in Rwanda in 1994. Kofi Annan, the Secretary-General of the United Nations said: "The success of this court in prosecuting genocide is a historic milestone and a defining example of the ability of the United Nations to create institutions which fulfil the highest aspirations of mankind."

Boys accused of genocide assembled in Kigali central prison, Rwanda

EXTRADITION

Extradition is a request from one government to another to return people suspected or convicted of crimes to the country that wants to try them or punish them. The increasing number of extradition treaties between countries means that there are fewer safe havens left for fugitives from justice. However, requests for extradition are not always satisfied. Great Britain's request to Brazil to return the Great Train robber, Ronald Biggs, was turned down on the grounds that, after twenty years, it was too late to bring him to justice.

In 1998, the case of Augusto Pinochet raised the prospect that those who commit crimes against humanity could face justice in the future. General Pinochet became president of Chile in 1973, after taking control of the country in a military coup. During his tenure until 1990, Pinochet was reputed to be responsible for the murder, torture, and disappearance of thousands of Chileans. In 1998 he was arrested in Great Britain, pending extradition for trial in Spain. His case may prompt host governments to think again before giving shelter to former leaders who may bring them legal and political embarrassment. And political leaders will be forced to consider their own actions, in the knowledge that they may be more likely to be held to account for them. During the century, a long list of tyrants—among them Pol Pot in Cambodia, Idi Amin in Uganda, and Suharto in Indonesia—could have been called to account if the international community had been authorized to act against them.

Augusto Pinochet in 1977. In 1973 he led a coup that ousted, and resulted in the death of, the Marxist president, Salvador Allende. He was the subject of an extradition case from Great Britain in the late 1990s.

During the next century, this could well be the case. The emergence of an international judicial order based on a near universal application of extradition should ensure that there are no hiding places for those whom the civilized international community considers to be criminals. The International Court of Justice will need to enforce its rulings if it is to continue to have any power and effect in the international arena. An international consensus, both legal and political, needs to exist to ensure that the worst atrocities do not go unpunished.

In the twentieth century, the war on crime and the consideration of appropriate methods of punishment have taken center stage in the minds of policymakers and public servants. "Law and order" has become a potent theme in political campaigns, and candidates who embrace it are more likely to be accepted by voters. However, it is increasingly obvious that there are no easy solutions to the problem of crime; and policies to tackle crime and impose punishment cannot be accomplished at a small cost, either economically or socially.

OPINION

"This is a defining moment in the effort to end impunity for international crimes." Michael Posner, the executive director of the Lawyers' Committee for Human Rights, commenting on the ruling that Augusto Pinochet be extradited to Spain. However, in December 1998, the ruling to extradite Pinochet was set aside.

An Indonesian prisoner is released from Cipinang prison in China in a Chinese independence day amnesty.

GLOSSARY

acquit to find a person not guilty of a crime.

amnesty a general pardon for crimes committed in the past. Amnesty allows the perpetrators to go unpunished.

anarchist a person who believes that governments and rules and regulations have no authority and who disobeys the law.

atone to make amends for a crime.

bootleg to make, carry, or sell illegal goods.

bribery giving money or a gift to induce someone to do something.

capitalism an economic system based on the private ownership of land and industry, in which most people work for wages.

colonize to extend control over other people or areas; historically, colonies had no real independence and were used by the colonial powers to gain access to raw materials and markets for exports.

coup an abbreviation of coup d'état—the sudden seizure of government by unelected people, usually the military.

courier a person who delivers an urgent message or package.

court-martial a special court for the trial of members of the military forces.

defendant a person accused of a crime.

democracy a political system in which the rulers of a state are elected by the people they rule through a process of voting.

embezzlement the dishonest conversion of property or money entrusted to one for one's own use.

extortion the securing of money, favors, and so on, by intimidation or violence.

extradition the surrender of an alleged offender to the state or country in whose territory the alleged offense took place.

federal describing a system of government in which several states with separate, local laws relate to a central government with national laws.

fraud obtaining money by deceiving people.

fundamentalism a belief in the literal truth of a religion.

genocide the deliberate and systematic destruction of a national, racial, religious, or ethnic group.

guerrilla a resistance fighter, usually working within a small group, attacking better-equipped enemy forces.

heterosexual a person who is sexually attracted to someone of the opposite sex.

hierarchical system a system in which people are organized by rank, with those above giving orders to those below.

homosexual a person who is sexually attracted to someone of the same sex.

joy-riding taking a stolen car and driving it recklessly for fun.

loan-sharking lending money to people at exorbitant rates of interest.

mugging attacking someone suddenly, with the intention of robbing them.

narcotics pain-relieving and sleep-inducing drugs, such as heroin and opium, and other drugs that depress brain activity; the term is often used to mean "illegal drugs."

pedophilia a crime that involves adults having sex with children.

protection racket a system by which gangsters obtain money from business people by assuring them that their property will not be damaged if they pay protection.

rehabilitate to help a prisoner to prepare to fit in to society or a new job, by vocational guidance, retraining, or therapy.

sabotage secretly destroying or damaging equipment.

sanctions penalties imposed on people or countries, depriving them of some kind of privilege or service.

stalking the obsessive watching and following of a person, causing him or her distress and discomfort.

surveillance the close observation of a person, for example, a criminal, by the police.

syndicate a group of business enterprises or individuals organized to undertake a joint project.

totalitarianism a system of government in which all activities are controlled by an unelected leader.

tribunal a form of court or hearing, usually without a jury, where disputes can be resolved.

welfare state a system in which the government collects money in taxes to provide social security for the less well-off.

BOOKS TO READ

Cooper, Alison. *A Punishment to Fit the Crime?*
Danbury, CT: Franklin Watts, 1997.

D'Angelo, Laura. *Hate Crimes* (Crime, Justice,
and Punishment). Broomall, PA: Chelsea
House, 1998.

Gottfried, Ted. *Capital Punishment: The Death
Penalty Debate* (Issues in Focus). Springfield,
NJ: Enslow Publishers, 1997.

Henson, Burt M. *Furman vs. Georgia: The Death
Penalty and the Constitution* (Historic Supreme
Court Cases). Danbury, CT: Franklin Watts,
1996.

Roden, Katie. *Solving International Crime*
(Crimebusters). Ridgefield, CT: Copper Beech
Books, 1996.

Steins, Richard. *The Death Penalty: Is It Justice?*
(Issues of Our Time). New York: 21st Century
Books, 1995.

Wolf, Robert V. *Capital Punishment* (Crime,
Justice, and Punishment). Broomall, PA:
Chelsea House, 1997.

USEFUL ADDRESSES

The following organizations are likely to provide either further information or educational material for young people and their teachers.

American Society of Criminology
1314 Kinnear Road
Columbus
Ohio 43212-1156
Email: asc41@compuserve.com

National Center for Juvenile Justice
701 Forbes Avenue
Pittsburgh, PA 15219
(412) 227-6950

National Crime Prevention Council
733 15th Street NW, Suite 540
Washington, DC 20005
(202) 466-6272

The Rand Corporation
2100 M Street NW
Washington, DC 20037
The Rand Corporation publishes the journal
Studies in Conflict and Terrorism

INDEX